The Economics of the Firm